The First Voyage: November 28, 1777; Congress elected John Adams Esqr a Commissioner to the Court of France to negotiate the affairs of America at this very critical period. Johnny Adams, on his own plea, would go with him.

THE MOMENTOUS OFFICE OF PEACE-MAKER

The Second Voyage to France, which halted in Spain: (John Adams was) elected September 27, 1779 minister plenipotentiary to negotiate treaties of peace and commerce with his Britannic Majesty, with Mr. Thaxter my private secretary, my two sons, John, twelve years old, and Charles, nine, and Mr. Dana, a gentleman of principal rank in this country and a member of Congress, and servants. Nov. 5, 1779

| Charley
born 1770 | Abigail 2
born 1765 | John, JA, born 1735 | Abigail, AA
born 1744 | John Q, JQA
born 1767 | Tommy
born 1772 |

The greatest pleasure I had in life,
the society of my children. *JA*

As in the beginning of the American Revolution, the ending of it was on John Adams' shoulders. Their ship *La Sensible* was sinking and just made it to Spain. For Adams it was "a great embarrassment," as he was desperate to reach Paris to end the war—which he did, by the bye, and wonderfully well. Much of the overland trip with his boys was on the great Pilgrim Road, the *Camino* to Santiago de Compostela. The hike or bike ride along the camino today is a truly uplifting historical and spiritual adventure. You can do it in installments. You can also ride on horseback or muleback, as in the days of the story following.

THE FIRST VOYAGE, Feb. 18–Mar. 31, 1778

Upon the mighty waters. *AA*

Captain Samuel Tucker, Commander of the Frigate *Boston,* with John Quincy Adams, eleven years of age. I had been led to (bring) my son with me, by his inclination and by the advice of all my friends. Mr. Johnny's behavior gave me a satisfaction, that I cannot express. Fully sensible of our danger, he was constantly endeavoring to bear up under it with a manly courage...

A thunder bolt struck...*JA* within a few inches of the Powder Room. *AA*

My little son was very proud of his knowledge of all the sails, and the Captain put him upon learning the Mariner's Compass. Mar. 5

Cover: Johnny wore a blue coat in his first portrait, and the boys wore blue coats later at college. Brother Tommy wore a blue coat to his father's Presidential Ball.

BACK TO BOSTON, June 17, 1779

By the gracious invitation of the king (of France), I am now to take passage in his frigate the *Sensible*, with his new ambassador to America, the Chevalier de La Luzerne. The chevalier and Secretary Marbois are in raptures with my son. He teaches them English, and corrects the pronunciation of every word and syllable and letter. (Earlier, waiting for the chevalier to sail to America) all day reading *Don Quixote*.

GOOD NEWS!
Les Espagnols viennent de se déclarer
...war against Great Britain. June 21

La libertad, Sancho, es uno de los más preciosos dones que a los hombres dieron los cielos...
Don Quixote, II, 58

Liberty, Sancho, is one of the most precious gifts which Heaven has bestowed upon men...

They arrived at their home in Braintree, near Boston, August 2. Drafting a frame of government (a constitution) for his state became Papa Adams' chief chore until he was sent again by Congress to France, to end the war. John Adams had studied the achievements of Don Quixote for years.

ABOARD THE FRENCH FRIGATE *LA SENSIBLE* AGAIN, A SALUTE!

On the 13th day of November, 1779, we went to Boston and embarked (two days later) on board the frigate whose yards were manned in honor of the passengers.

French flags, right: top, *azure* (blue), fleurs-de-lis, *or* (gold); bottom, *argent* (white).

OH, OH! A LEAK IN *LA SENSIBLE*

We set two pumps to work. This brought the Captain, Officers and Passengers to them in their turn. *Dana*

Nov. 25, 1779

We had not been two days at sea before I perceived that the pumps were going and that a leak in the ship was constantly admitting a great deal of water...it constantly increased from day to day, the pumps were worked by day and night, till all the people on board, passengers and officers as well as (350) seamen, were almost exhausted with fatigue. The *Sensible* was an old frigate, and her planks and timbers were so decayed, that one half the violence of winds and waves which had so nearly wrecked the new and strong ship the *Boston* the year before would have torn her to pieces. The captain determined to put into Spain...Dec. 8, we got into Ferrol.

What Mariner is not afraid
To venture in a ship decayed?
Dr. Swift

The Toil, the Danger of the Seas;
Great Ministers ne'er think of these.
Dr. Swift

Before we entered the harbor we were obliged to set a third pump to work and for the greater part of the time since her arrival in the harbor four pumps have been going and our ship makes 7½ feet of water in one hour. We have great reason therefore to thank heaven for safe arrival in this place. *Dana*   A crazy, leaky ship. *Thaxter*

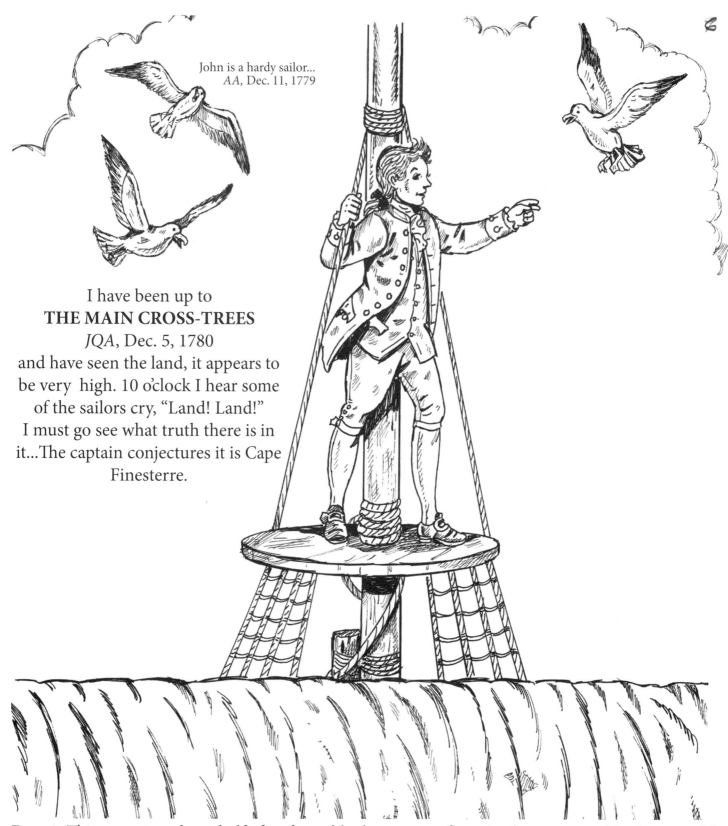

John is a hardy sailor...
AA, Dec. 11, 1779

I have been up to
THE MAIN CROSS-TREES
JQA, Dec. 5, 1780
and have seen the land, it appears to
be very high. 10 o'clock I hear some
of the sailors cry, "Land! Land!"
I must go see what truth there is in
it...The captain conjectures it is Cape
Finesterre.

Dec. 8. This morning about half after four o'clock we saw a fort. At about seven o'clock we could see her very plain, she hoists Spanish colors and we French ones and fired a gun...It is an amazing strong fort. In one of the forts there are 365 guns. The city of Ferrol, the harbor of which we are now in, is a small city but the houses appear from here well built. I thought the fort saluted us at twelve o'clock but I find it is the Spanish Admiral's birthday and they have a great festival of it. *JQA JA* to *AA*, Dec. 16. The frigate *La Sensible* is in so bad condition as to make it probable she will not be fit to put to sea...

MAKING ALLIANCE COCKADES, Dec.14, 1779

The officers here French and Spanish have a cockade red & white for the alliance between France & Spain. Captain Chavagnes desired all his officers to add the black to it and put one on himself...The Spanish and French officers wondered at it and enquired of the frigates officers what they had the black for. They told them that France being allied to the thirteen United States of America they put it in. For that reason, the captain said that it was only what was due for the politeness that he had been used with in Boston. There's an example of French compliments. *JQA*

A black cockade was an American symbol during the war and was later made an official War Department badge. Red was for Spain from the red cross of Burgundy. White was for France, from the Bourbon white flag.

DINING ABOARD THE *JASON*, FERROL, Dec. 10, 1779

A captain of one of the French Men of War very politely invited me to dine with him. My brother Charles and I went on board of the *Jason* of 64 guns. The captain and all the officers were all exceeding polite. *JQA* The *Jason* is taken. Jan. 19, 1780.

THE COMEDY, or ITALIAN OPERA, FERROL, Dec. 13, 1779

I have been to the play with Mr. Dana, Mr. Allen (a Boston merchant), Mr. Thaxter and my brother Charles. We saw there Captain Chavagnes and all the officers of the ship, and one from the *Jason*. There are some fine dancers there. *JQA*

You have entered early in life upon the great Theater of the world. *AA* to *JQA*, June 10, 1778

FERROL, Dec. 14, 1779

Finding that I must reside some weeks in Spain, I determined to acquire the language, to which purpose we went to a bookseller and purchased Sobrino's Dictionary in three vols. And the *Gramática Castellana,* which is an excellent Spanish grammar, in their own tongue, and also a Latin grammar in Spanish. By help of these books, the children are learning the language very fast.

A Treasure here of Learning lurks

Huge Heaps of never-dying Works.
Dr. Swift

The first step of the sciences is that of the languages...
El primer escalón de las ciencias es el de las lenguas. — DQ II, 16

TO LA CORUÑA
CROSSING THE HARBOR FROM FERROL
Dec. 15, 1779

This morning at 5 o'clock we dressed and drank a cup of chocolate. We then went down to the wharf and went on board a boat to cross over the other side of the bason. *JQA*

The Province of Galicia is one of the largest in Spain, and said to be one of the best peopled. Coruña is in effect the principal city, although St. Iago...is in name the capital. *JA*, Jan. 16, 1780

Prepare a fleet to waft him o' er, make Gulliver his Commodore.
Dr. Swift

To Abigail Adams: I assure you that it gave me the highest pleasure to see Mr. Adams treated with every mark of attention and respect at Ferrol by all ranks and the two children also on his and their own account; and did they know the good sense, merits and accomplishments of their Mama, they would experience additional tokens of both. *Thaxter*, this date.

I have really no right to quarrel with old Neptune, since he has three times safely transported my friend. Though he has grumbled and growled, he has not shown the extent of his power. *AA*

Left, Arms of La Coruña: sky *azure* (blue); waves wavy *azure* and *argent* (white); tower argent; scallop shells *or* (gold); king's head and hill *proper* (natural). Flags above: Galicia, foremast: field *azure*; chalice and crosslets *or*; Host (circle), *argent*. Aft: flag of the Naval Department of Ferrol: field *argent*; cross of Burgundy *gules* (red). Pope Alexander IV, 1254-1261, ruled that only pilgrims could bear scallop shells on their arms. This is the pilgrims' harbor as well as an historic naval base.

A CAVALCADE OF YANKEE DON QUIXOTES ON HOG BRIDGE
Ferrol to La Coruña, about 20 miles, Marching in Train
Dec. 15, 1779

When we arrived the muleteers were not quite ready but we soon got ready, and then we set out like so many Don Quixotes and Sancho Panzas. We were eleven in Company (plus the muleteers) and in this order: 1st the French Consul's servant, 2nd my papa, 3rd Mr. (secretary)Dana, 4th Mr. Allen (Boston merchant), 5th Mr. Thaxter (cousin, tutor, secretary), 6th Mr. Sam Cooper Johennot (age 11), 7th my brother Charles (age 9) & 8th myself who made the center, 9th the consul's servant, 10th Mr. Dana's servant, 11th and last the muleteer who brought up the rear. We passed several bridges and amongst the rest one of a mile long which they call Devil's Bridge and another (here) at which we dined which was called Hog's Bridge. Droll names for bridges, I think? We also passed over a number of prodigious high mountains. *JQA*

Who would not swear, when you contrive thus,
That you are not Don Quixote *Redivivus*?
Dr. Swift

We arrived at Coruña about seven o'clock and put up at the Hotel du Grand Amiral. An officer kept open the gate for us to enter, attended us to our lodgings, and then insisted on our visiting the general who is governor of the province and a colonel who is military governor of the town. They made many professions of friendship to our cause and country. *JA*

Dec. 16. This morning the governor of the Province of Galicia and the governor of the town of Coruña came to my lodgings (this compliment the general had not paid anyone before, *Dana*), invited me to dine with him tomorrow with all my family. He insisted upon seeing my sons. Said that he and everything in his power was at my service. I told him I was studying Spanish and hoped that the next time I should have the honor to see his excellency I should be able to speak to him in Spanish. He smiled and bowed. *JA*

**THE BOYS
MEET THE GENERAL**
La Coruña, Dec. 17, 1779

Don Pedro Martín Cermeño, the Governor of the Province of Galicia, or rather, the Vice Roy of the Kingdom of Galicia. He had orders from Court to treat all Americans as the best friends of Spain.

Sábete, Sancho, que no es un hombre más que otro si no hace más que otro... DQ I,18
Bear in mind, Sancho, that one man is no more than another unless he does more than another.

Galicia colors as before.
For more about Natural Equality, see JA to CA, Jan. 9, 22, Feb. 17, 24, 1794.

CHURCH OF SANTIAGO
(Saint James the Apostle)
La Coruña, Dec. 18, 1779
Walked all around the town. *JA*
Santiago is charging up above in
the tympanum. His adventures will
be told shortly, and lawyer Adams
will discusses an amazing legal
case. This is the oldest church in La
Coruña, built atop a Roman temple.

A CHOCOLATE PARTY
La Coruña, Dec. 22, 1779
Saw the ladies drink chocolate
in the Spanish fashion. To AA:
I have met with few things more
remarkable than the chocolate
which is the finest I ever saw.

Talents for
conversation fit,
Are humor, breeding,
sense and wit.
Dr. Swift

THE TOWER OF HERCULES, Dec. 17, 1779

Hercules, that my children should follow his example, is my earnest prayer. JA, 1780

Earlier: a Great Seal for the confederated States...I proposed the choice of Hercules...(Virtue vs. Sloth). Aug. 14, 1776

This is a very ancient monument. It is of stone an hundred foot high (actually 112). It was intended for a lighthouse, perhaps as it commands a very wide prospect of the sea. It sees all the vessels coming from the east and from the west. There was formerly a magnificent stair case, winding round it in a spiral from ground to top, and it is said that some general once rode to the top of it, in a coach, or on horse back. But the stairs are all taken away and the stones employed to pave the streets of Coruña. *JA*

There is an inscription which I have not seen for I could not go in, which runs thus: "Marti et Agusto Sacrum. Dedicated to Mars and Augustus." Dec. 20. I went to the (French) Consul's after the inscription...he had not got it yet but expected to have it today. Dec. 25. The Consul came here this evening and gave us the inscription (as more accurately, below). It was a monk who took the inscription from the rock some years agone. Perhaps the translation may not appear very elegant but the characters being effaced a great deal, the monk could not take down the whole of the inscription. *JQA*

I have translated it as well as I can. *JQA, Dec. 25*

We have placed the inscription where we imagine it may have been.

MARTI AVG SACR G SEVIVS LVPVS ARCHITECTVS AEMINIENSIS LVSITANVS EXV

G. Sevius Lupus, architect from Coimbra in Lusitania, dedicates (this) to Mars Augustus.

Hispania Epigraphica record 8369, CIL 2559

ON TOP OF THE TOWER
La Coruña, Dec. 21, 1779

Sammy Cooper (Johonnot, age 11, on his way to school in France), Charley & I went up to the top of the tower. Rained almost all the time. *JQA*

Sammy was the grandson of the Rev. Dr. Sam'l Cooper, John Adams' Boston pastor, who was a paid French agent and later befuddled JA . Mr. Thaxter wrote Abigail Adams, Dec. 16: "This genius (Sammy) is vain, he is rude, he is impudent. He is troublesome to the last degree...Charles has given him some severe rubs this evening. I can't deny, I enjoyed them." (We're glad this didn't happen up here.) Hercules, too had travelled to Spain, to collect cattle from a three-headed giant near Cádiz. Next he had to get the golden apples of the Hesperides in Africa, given to Hera by Zeus and guarded by a dragon with 100 heads. Crossing to Africa then was easy, for there was land all the way. When he saw how close the ocean was to the Mediterranean Sea, he opened a gap between Europe and Africa; ships could now go from one to the other. He wanted to leave something to mark this farthest spot of his travels; the mountains on each side of the strait became the Pillars of Hercules. This tower, built by Herculean engineers also in ancient days, aided Roman ships using Hercules' gap to explore, conquer and trade, and has since helped Vikings, Crusaders, fisher-folk and Armadas of many ages. *Ed.*

From a model in the Museo Histórico Militar de La Coruña.
President Adams, Father of our Navy, said, 1799, "May every ship prove a pillar of Hercules."

A part of an
IRISH BATTALION OF TROOPS
La Coruña, Dec. 17, 1779

before the court house made a fine appearance. There are six battalions of Irish troops in Spain, in three regiments, several of whose officers have visited me to assure me of their respects to the United States. *JA*

There are 50,000 men in arms in Ireland all united in the generous intention of freeing themselves from the yoke of that tyrant George the 3d. *JQA,* Jan. 19, 1780

HIBERNIA

The governor of the town of Coruña, Colonel Patricio O'Hara, is an Irish gentleman. *JA*

Early Irish mythology of the Gaelic Milesians (from *Mil Espaine,* Soldier of Spain) from La Coruña, had long connected the two countries.

Flag: field *argent* (white); cross of Burgundy *gules* (red); harp *or* (gold) on *azure* (blue). Colonel & troops: red coats & breeches, blue waistcoats, white leggings.

Three Boston Lawyers Visit
THE COURT HOUSE, LA CORUÑA, Dec. 20, 1779

Went to the Audiencia, where we saw four judges sitting in their robes... nearly like ours in Boston.

Thaxter

Dana

JA

Cuando la justicia estuviese en duda, me decantase y acogiese a la misericordia.
DQ II, 51. When justice is in doubt, I should lean on the side of mercy.

CHRISTMAS, LA CORUÑA, 1779

Went to the palace, at 11 o'clock, to take my leave of his excellency. The general repeated a thousand obliging things. *JA*

The general had before sent us a passport through the kingdom requiring all civil officers, &c., to cause us to be supplied with every convenience we might need and at the prices stipulated for the Royal Service. He again assured us of his readiness to give us any further assistance, and in particular he offered us an escort of horse or foot (soldiers) if we should choose, to attend us on our journey through the kingdom...to this courtly offer, as courtly a reply was made as could be expected of staunch American Republicans. *Dana*

Having been detained at Coruña ten full days, when we did not intend to have spent more than one, waiting with the utmost impatience for mules and calashes (carriages) to proceed on our journey, and having sent to Lugo and to Santiago to procure them, we at last by the special assistance of Mr. Lagoanere (American agent, a very worthy merchant of this place), got them and we began our journey. *Dana*

BOARDING OUR CARRIAGE
La Coruña, Dec. 26, 1779

There were three carriages all drawn by mules, two at each carriage, each carries two persons, except one which carries three. The three servants rode a mule back as also did our guide. In the first carriage was Mr. Allen (Boston merchant) and Sammy Cooper. One of their mules had near a hundred little bells tied round its neck. Next Mr. Dana, and Mr. Thaxter, one of theirs had some bells but not many, And lastly my Papa, brother Charles and myself. Neither of our mules had any bells. Mr. Lagoanere rode on a horse belonging to him. And thus equipped, our caravan set out. Our first stage was 12 miles off of Coruña (four leagues); at about 7 o'clock we arrived at a village called Betanzos, formerly the capital of the province of Galicia which is to this day called the Kingdom of Galicia. This is also the place where the archives of this province are kept.

JQA

Blue wheels, light blue coach, gilt trim (Goya).

Mr. Lagoanere made us the compliment to attend us to this place. The house, the beds and the people appeared to me too romantic for description. *JA*

Dec. 27. 'Tis time to get up. If the guide had not have kept his time the bells of the church would have kept the time for him. For about a quarter of an hour after we got up they began to ring and rung for about half an hour. *JQA*

SANTIAGO de BETANZOS, Dec. 26, 1779
We have right against our lodgings this large church. *JQA*
Mr. Lagoanere tells the story of Santiago, riding above in the tympanum, adored at Clavijo.

SANTIAGO CHURCH, BETANZOS, Dec. 27, 1779

Mr. Lagoanere told us that the original of the shrine and temple of Santiago (next page) was this. A certain Shepherd (Pelagius) saw a bright light there in the night. Afterwards it was revealed that St. James was buried there. This laid the foundation of a church, and they have built an altar (in 813) on the spot where the shepherd saw the light. In the time of the Moors, the people made a vow, that if the Moors should be driven from this country, they would give a certain portion of the income of their lands to St. James. The Moors were defeated (at the Battle of Clavijo, 844) and it was reported and believed that Saint James was in the battle and fought with a drawn sword at the head of the Spanish troops, on horseback. The people, believing that they owed the victory to the Saint, very cheerfully fulfilled their vows by paying the tribute.

But lately, a descendant of the famous duke (of Alba, who lost the Spanish Netherlands to William the Silent in 1573), has refused to pay for his estate, which occasioned a law suit, which is carried by appeal to Rome. The duke attempted to prove that St. James was never in Spain. The pope has suspended the cause. Great numbers of pilgrims visit Santiago de Compostela every year, from France, Spain, Italy and other parts of Europe (and today, from America), many of them on foot.

I have always regretted that we
could not find time to make a
Pilgrimage to
SANTIAGO de COMPOSTELA.
John Adams

Funded in 1075 by Alfonso VI
with tribute from Granada;
built by Bishop Peláez and
Archbishop Gelmírez.

SANTIAGO PEREGRINO
as a pilgrim, from the Puerta Santa
Santiago de Compostela Cathedral

The Pilgrim Song

Who would true Valour see,
Let him come hither;
One here will Constant be,
Come Wind, come Weather.
There's no *Discouragement*,
Shall make him once *Relent*,
His first avow'd *Intent*,
To be a Pilgrim.

Who so beset him round,
With dismal *Stories*,
Do but themselves Confound;
His Strength the *more is*.
No *Lyon* can him fright
He'll with a *Gyant Fight*
But he will have a right
To be a Pilgrim.

Hobgoblin, nor foul *Fiend*,
Can *daunt* his Spirit:
He knows, he *at the end*,
Shall Life Inherit.
Then Fancies fly away,
He'll fear not what men say,
He'll labour Night and Day,
To be a Pilgrim.

John Bunyan, 1684

*Santiago de Compostela—Campus Stellae—*Saint James of the Field of Stars: while some said that Pelagius saw a star in A.D. 813, others said that Charlemagne's dream of the Milky Way led to finding Saint James the Apostle's grave at a place that had been called *Libredón* (gift, of Queen Lupa). 800 years earlier, Saint James had preached in Spain, it was thought. He returned to the Holy Land, was beheaded in A.D. 44, then was put onto a boat made of stone. It sailed to Spain, to Iria Flavia, now Padrón, in Galicia, and then he went to his grave inland, in what was later called the Field of Stars. Legends, like "ballads, are too old to lie," said Sancho Panza. *DQ* II. 33.

We struggled patiently and perseveringly
LIKE RESOLUTE PILGRIMS, *Thaxter*

...and very frequently we were all
obliged to walk as much more safe
and agreeable than carriages or saddles.

We travelled from Betanzos to Castillano. The roads are mountainous and rocky. Neither the horses nor the mules could be trusted, in ascending or descending the rocky steeps of the mountains in the carriages without two men on foot to hold them by their bridles and their heads, and with all our precautions, we broke one of our axle trees, early in the day...The house in Castillano where we lodged was of stone, two stories in height. We entered into the kitchen, where was no floor but the ground and no carpet but straw trodden into mire by men, hogs, horses, mules, etc. In the middle of the kitchen was a mound raised a little above the level of the ground with stones and earth, on which was a fire, with pots, kettles, skillets &c, of the fashion of the country over it, and round about it. On one side was a flue oven, very large, black, smoky and sooty. On the opposite side of the fire was a cabin filled with straw where I suppose the *patrón de la casa,* that is, the master of the house, his wife and four children all lodged and slept together.

On the same floor with the kitchen was the stable. There was a flight of steps from the kitchen floor up into a chamber, on the left hand was a stage, on which was a bed of straw and on the straw lay a fatting hog. Around the kitchen fire were arranged the man and woman of the house, four children, all the travellers, servants, muleteers &c. Over the fire was a very large kettle full of turnips and onions, very large and very fine boiling for the food of all the family of men and beasts inhabiting both the kitchen and the stable, and the stage.

THE DINING ROOM AT CASTILLANO, Dec. 27, 1779

SANTIAGO
de BAAMONDE, Dec. 28

From Betanzos to Castillano the road is very rocky and hilly, except the first part of it. You ascend two very long and high hills, which are almost impassible with carriages; we had two calashes drawn by two mules each, they were overturned three or four times upon the last hill and the axle-tree of one of them broken down amidst a heavy rain. *Dana*

We went to see the
CATHEDRAL (of SANTA MARÍA) at LUGO
which is very rich. Dec. 30, 1779

From Baamonde to Lugo, which is a city, the road was still better. From Lugo to Gallego to O Cebreiro, from the foot of the mountains, you almost constantly rise for several leagues, mountain after mountain and when you have ascended to the pinnacle (O Cebreiro) it may be said you enter the region of the gods. When we passed a mountain about two miles short of O Cebreiro on all sides there opened upon us a prospect the most sublime imagination can conceive...It must be seen to be felt— here was such a magnificent display of the great works of nature's God as filled the soul with astonishment and veneration. *Dana*

Lugo, Astorga, León and Burgos Cathedrals and others are named for Santa María, who had aided Pelayo the Visigoth to victory in the legendary battle of Covadonga in 722. She is also the protectress of pilgrims and sailors.

GALLEGO Dec. 30, 1779

We went from Lugo to Gallego and arrived in very good season...the road was mountainous but not rocky...We passed over a large bridge over a river (Neira) called Carracedo
which empties itself into the Minho not far from Lugo...We are obligated, in
this journey, to carry our own beds, blankets, sheets, pillows &c., our
own provisions of chocolate, tea, sugar, meat, wine, spirits,
and every thing that we want. We carry our own but-
ter, cheese, and indeed salt and pepper too. *JA*

O CEBREIRO, NEW YEAR'S EVE, 1779

We are now on the highest ground of all. JA

The day was fine, and the sunshine in all his glory, and was just about to close the scene. Having happily arrived to this most remarkable point of this world, we closed the year this evening with joy and gratitude. The next morning (January 1, 1780) was as fine as we could hope for; thus favored with respect to the weather (for our station was very critical), we began our progress down the mountains. The first we descended was very long, steep and difficult of passage; the road being rocky, and running upon the edge of enormous precipices, that the accident of overturning a carrriage or startling a mule on one side, would have hurled us to the bottom of

creation. We didn't choose to hazard this, and therefore dismounted. At the foot of this mountain begins the Province of León and all danger of travelling here ceases. The distance from the pinnacle to Villafranca del Bierzo is seven leagues (about 21 miles); the road runs in a beautiful serpentine manner between the mountains, which are so near together that the interval which lies beneath them is not upon average ⅛ of a mile wide and is a good made road. *Dana*

Jan.1, 1780. Mr. Thaxter woke me up by sounding in my ear, "I wish you a Happy New Year," and about half an hour before sunrise we set off from Cebreiro. At about 5 o'clock we arrived at a city called Villafranca del Bierzo where we log'd tonight. As we were coming along we saw an ancient castle of the Moors and right over against us there is a castle of one of the lords before the use of muskets was known. *JQA*

VILLAFRANCA DEL BIERZO, Jan. 1, 1780

The road at first was steep, sharp pitches, ragged rocks, &c. We then came into the road of León, which is made seemingly out of rock. It was an excellent road for a league and a half. We then came to a river, and travelled along the banks of it. Miry, rocky, up and down until we came into a new road. Here we found a road again made entirely by art, at an immense expense, but seems to be made forever. The work is an honor to the nation. It shows that improvements are coming in, and attention is paid to the ease, convenience, utility, commerce, &c. of the people. This evening I bought a mule, saddle, bridle &c. for 62 dollars and a half.

Santiago
Church

The country we have travelled over today is the greatest curiosity I ever beheld - an uninterrupted succession of mountains of a vast height. The River Valcarce flows between two rows of mountains, rising on each hand to a vast height. The most grand, sublime, awful objects, yet they are cultivated up to their highest summits. There are flourishing fields of grain, on such steep declivities, near the summits of mountains, as I cannot conceive it possible for horses or cattle to stand upon them to plough. It must be done with mules.

PONFERRADA, Jan. 2, 1780
Iron Bridge

We passed through several villages of which Ponferrada was the most considerable and has an ancient castle. *Dana*
This was a former Roman fort, rebuilt by the Knights Templar in 1218. Ages of weary pilgrims to Santiago de Compostela were protected from here. There are 2,500 or more castles in Spain, many quite splendid to see.

The castle has a double gate; the first is defended by two strong towers, the 2nd is higher, and enters into the *patio de armas*. It is considered the most important castle in the north of Spain. *Ed.*

SPENT THE NIGHT IN BEMBIBRE

Jan. 2, 1780 We set off from Bembibre for Astorga and passed through the village by the light of a candle. *Dana*   We met coaches and genteel people as we went into Astorga. *JA*

San Pedro

Ladies rode behind their squires.
Las señoras iban a las ancas de sus escuderos. DQ II, 48

Cathedral SANTA MARÍA de ASTORGA, Jan. 4
The most magnificent I have yet seen in Spain. *JA*

About 12 o'clock I with Mr. Dana, Mr. Thaxter and Sammy Johonnot went to see the cathedral but the man was gone to dinner and the door was shut.
JQA
Later: a grand building, both within and without and particularly within, it surpasses any I have yet seen.
Dana

Thaxter

Sammy

JQA

Dana

THE WALLS OF ASTORGA

Jan. 4, 1780

Walked twice round the walls of the city, which are very ancient. Saw the road of León and Bay-onne, and the road to Madrid. There is a pleasant prospect of the country from the walls. *JA*

At Astorga we determined not to go to Madrid. (At Burgos) we will determine to go to Bilbao or directly to Bayonne (in France). *JQA*

Saw the market of vegetables. The onions and turnips were the largest and finest I ever saw. The cabbages, carrots &c. Saw the market of fuel-wood, turf and brush. Saw numbers of Maragato women (Berber descendants, muleteers' wives). Crucifixes, beads and chains, earrings and finger-rings in silver, brass, glass &c. about their necks &c. Saw the Parliament House or *Casa de la Ciudad* where the Corregidor and city magistrates assemble, to deliberate and to execute the orders of the king. *JA*

THE MARKET AT ASTORGA, Jan. 4, 1780
Orange skirts, scarlet crossovers

TO LEÓN, Jan. 5, 1780

Rode from Astorga to León eight leagues. This is one great plain. The road very fine. Great flocks of sheep and cattle. The sheep of handsome size, the fleeces of wool thick, long and extremely fine. We passed several small villages. The vast range of Asturias Mountains covered with snow on our left. The weather as pleasant as could be - though cold - some frost and ice on the roads.

Saliendo de entre unos árboles, dos hermosísimas pastoras...DQ II, 58
From among some trees two shepherdesses of surpassing beauty presented themselves...

We passed the
RIVER AND BRIDGE ÓRBIGO, Jan. 5, 1780,
which in the spring, when swelled with freshets of melted snow from the mountains of Asturias, is a very great river. León, which we entered in the night, has the appearance of a large city.

EL PASO HONROSO

Don Suero de Quiñones of León vowed before the king and queen to hold this bridge for 30 days, with nine companions, July 10 to August 9, 1434, until he had fought with lance against 300 knights who refused to admit the pre-eminent beauty of his lady-love, Doña Leonor de Tovar. Santiago was his witness. It was a Jubilee year (when Santiago's Day, July 25, falls on a Sunday), and many knights were travelling to Santiago de Compostela over the bridge. Later, Don Suero was wounded and became himself a pilgrim to Santiago. There, still in the cathedral, lies the blue ribbon Doña Leonor had given Don Suero as a token. Don Quixote admired this story. *Ed.*

SANTA MARÍA de LEÓN, *Jan. 6, 1780*

Built 1065–1073

We went to see the cathedral...
magnificent. *JA* This day is the
Feast of the King; there was a
procession of the bishop and
clergy preceeded with music of
French horns
and violins.
Dana

Happy Birthday Don Carlos III: the King of Spain (& the Californias) will be 64. *JQA*
He sent George Washington a fine donkey, *Royal Gift*, father of mules in the USA.

Announcing the birth of Jesus to the shepherds.

ANGE LVS A PAS TORES

THE PANTHEON OF THE KINGS OF SAN ISIDORO, LEÓN
Saw the old castle of King Alfonso. *JA*, Jan. 6

King Ferdinand I of Castile married Sancha of León and so became king of both in 1038. Sancha's father, Alfonso V, was in the royal cemetery in León, and she with King Ferdinand established a new church for the burial of the kings and queens of her family. The church was dedicated in 1063. Their daughter Urraca carried on the work of her mother in building up the new church, called San Isidoro from the great and learned Bishop of Seville in the seventh century, before the Moors' conquest there. His sacred bones were brought to León to be interred in the new church. Urraca expanded the church to include the Pantheon of the Kings, which was decorated about 1180 by a French painter with lively and gorgeous frescos of biblical scenes on the walls and ceiling. So wonderful were the pictures that it has been called the "Sistine Chapel of the Romanesque period." Urraca's brother became King Alfonso VI in 1065 and his daughter, also Urraca, became queen in 1109. She and her daughter Sancha added to the church, too. *Ed.*

THE FANDANGO, Jan. 6, 1780

We passed thro several very little villages, in every one of which we saw the young people men and women dancing a dance they call the fandango. One of the young women beats a machine, somewhat like a section of a drum. It is covered with parchment. She sings and beats on her drum, and the company dance, with each a pair of clackers in his and her hand. The clackers are two pieces of wood, cut handsomely enough, which they have the art to rattle in their hands to the time of the drum.

Come, and trip it as ye go
On the light fantastic toe,
And in thy right hand lead with thee
The Mountain Nymph, sweet Liberty...
Milton

Atop a tower at
MANSILLA DE LAS MULAS,
Jan. 6, 1780

Ye old mule, that think yourself so fair,
Leave off with craft your beauty to repair...
Sir Thomas Wyatt

This was once a walled city. The towers were yet standing all around the town, and ruins and fragments of the wall, and the appearance of a foss around it still remain. We went to the top of one of the towers, from which we had a full view of the town.

Arco de San Benito
SAN JUAN SAHAGÚN
Jan. 7, 1780
-the greatest monastery of the realm, and pantheon of the royal family. Alfonso VI, who reunited and expanded the kingdom of Leon-Castile, died in 1109 and was buried here and succeeded by his daughter, the indomitable Queen Urraca. She followed his policy,

battling husband el Batallador of Aragón, sister Theresa of Portugal, son, who became Alfonso VII in 1126. We imagine these uniters of the kingdom of Castile and León welcoming a fellow uniter, John Adams, who did so much to unite 13 oppressed American colonies, now states, then desperately at war. *Ed.*

King Alfonso VI made Sahagún the headquarters of Abbot Bernard of Cluny, who soon after was promoted to Archbishop of Toledo. Monks of Cluny had prayed for Alfonso earlier, that he be freed from the prison where Sancho his brother had put him—and it worked. *Ed.*

Santa Eulalia Church
PAREDES DE NAVA, Jan. 8, 1780
Rode here from San Juan Sahagún. From Paredes we set off at 8 o'clock and reached Palencia, 4 leagues, at 12 o'clock where we dined. Palencia is a walled town and the most considerable one for size. We left Palencia at 2 o'clock and got into Torquemada 3 leagues a little after dark. We yesterday crossed a new canal making by the king, but lost the course of it, but this morning we met with it again.
Dana

Jan. 9, 1780: Mr. Dana explains
THE CANAL OF ARAGÓN, FROM SEA TO SEA
designed to form a communication by the Ebro River between
Santander in the Bay of Biscay to Tortosa on the borders of the Mediterranean.

The canal of Old Castile begins at Segovia and is separated from the southern canal by the chain of mountains. From Segovia, quitting the Eresma, it crosses the Pisuerga, near Valladolid at the junction of that river with the Duero, then leaving Palencia with the Carrión to the right, till it has crossed that river below Herrera, it approaches once more the Pisuerga, near Herrera.

As Rivers tho', they bend and twine,
Still to the Sea their Course incline.
Dr. Swift

Spain knew the importance of inland waterways. She was friendly to America because the kings of France and Spain were both in the Bourbon family, and France was fighting for us. But Spain wouldn't make a treaty with us without the Mississippi River. Johnny Adams would have much to do with this when he was Secretary of State, in 1817. Spain claimed the whole territory westward from Louisiana; their province of Texas extended to the Mississippi, and the waters of the Mississippi were always within the line of Spanish dominion, they said. But you know how it worked out. *Ed.*

San Antolín
CATHEDRAL OF PALENCIA
where Queen Doña Urraca lies.
Jan. 8, 1780

A Very Significant Event

Here, Oct. 25, 1113, a Council with Urraca, just victorious in capturing Burgos from El Batallador's forces, met with many bishops, abbots, dukes, princes, counts, magnates, to discuss Peace. *Reilly*

Above Palencia is a branch going westward to Zamora making this canal in its whole extent 140 leagues. They have already completed 20 leagues of it, with 24 locks, 3 bridges for aqueducts some ½ league through a high mountain. It has cost 38,000,000 reals or 180,000 pounds sterling (a lot of money). The dimensions are 9 feet deep, 20 feet wide at bottom and 60 feet inside at top. At Reinosa is the communication with the Canal of Aragón.

WE PASSED THROUGH A VILLAGE EVERY LEAGUE, Jan. 8, 1780

We met a good deal of frost and ice in the road. Our mules found more difficulty to keep their steps firm upon the ice than they had among the roughest rocks in the mountains. *JA*

Carrión de los Condes and Frómista were right on the Camino de Santiago, which the Adamses had been following. Carrión is on a hill, surely now a slippery one. They went below the Camino, to Palencia. They did not list every hamlet they passed, but if they missed these two, they missed true wonders. The first town had been renamed after the sons of King Alfonso VI, who were *condes,* counts, of Carrión. *El Cid* (Lord) *Campeador* (fighter) had captured Valencia in 1094, and the king bade his sons to marry the Cid's daughters. This plot is fiction, thank goodness: the bad sons treated the girls horribly on the way home. This

From a frieze in Santiago Church, Carrión de los Condes

infuriated both king and Cid, so a knightly trial of the condes with lance and sword was ordered. The Cid's champions had their hero's great swords, *Colada* and *Tizón.* In the end, the girls made more worthy marriages and became queens of Navarre and Aragón. *Ed.*

San Martín de Frómista, begun by Doña Mayor, widow of Sancho el Mayor, King of Navarre, in 1035.
It is called the most beautiful Romanesque church in Spain.

TORQUEMADA, Jan. 10, 1780

Torquemada is pretty enough to deserve a gentler name. Wigram

We set off from Torquemada before sunrise. We crossed the river again over another new stone bridge of 18 arches and crossed a river over a very fine new bridge of 15 arches. The canal mentioned before is let into this river which goes to Burgos, about two leagues further. *Dana*

THE FAMOUS CITY OF BURGOS →

THE ANCIENT CAPITAL OF THE RENOWNED KINGDOM OF CASTILE, Jan. 11, 1780

The next stage we rode eight leagues to Celada del Camino by 5 o'clock, the road being good the whole way. We left Celada before sunrise and got into Burgos about ½ past 11 o'clock. After dinner we walked about the city & went to see the cathedral church which in extent and the number of chapels in it exceeds any we have seen. The city has more good buildings in it than the others we have passed through. This seemed to be a place of some business. *Dana*

No Chimneys, No Trees: John Adams noted frequently that their lodgings did not have chimneys. Unlike New England, Spain lacked great supplies of firewood. What they had was necessary for cooking, and the heat from that was all the houses had. There were fuel sellers on market days, and collectors of twigs supplied them like this.

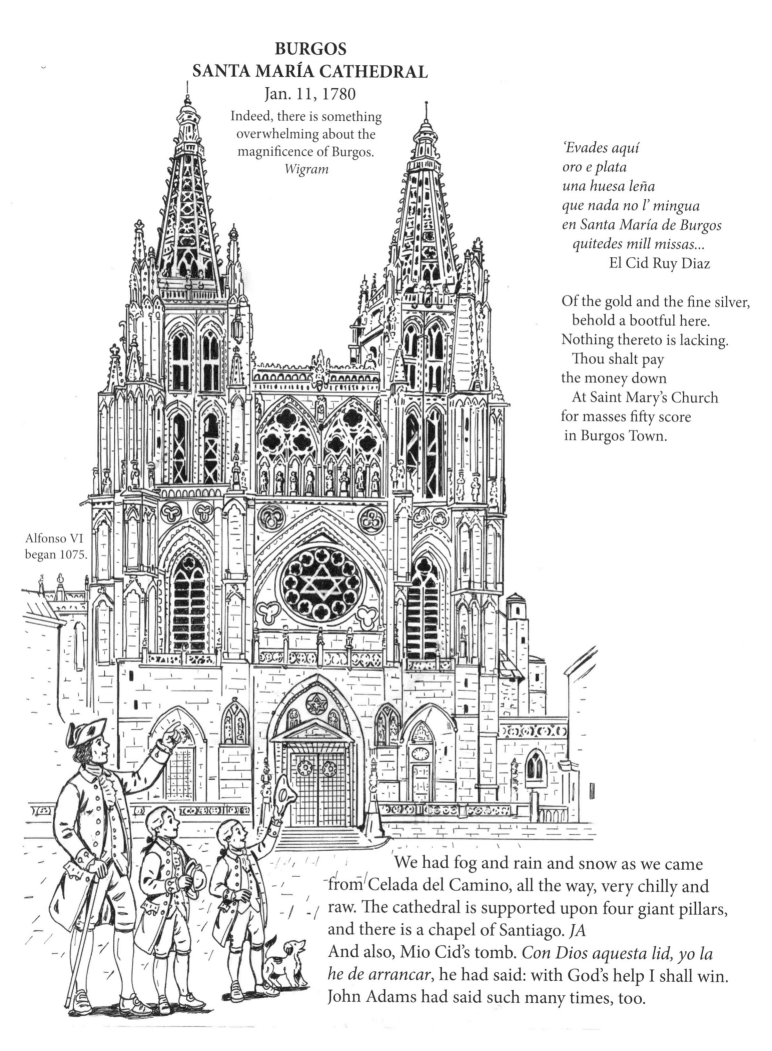

BURGOS
SANTA MARÍA CATHEDRAL
Jan. 11, 1780

Indeed, there is something
overwhelming about the
magnificence of Burgos.
Wigram

Alfonso VI
began 1075.

'Evades aquí
oro e plata
una huesa leña
que nada no l' mingua
en Santa María de Burgos
quitedes mill missas...
El Cid Ruy Diaz

Of the gold and the fine silver,
 behold a bootful here.
Nothing thereto is lacking.
 Thou shalt pay
the money down
 At Saint Mary's Church
for masses fifty score
 in Burgos Town.

We had fog and rain and snow as we came
from Celada del Camino, all the way, very chilly and
raw. The cathedral is supported upon four giant pillars,
and there is a chapel of Santiago. *JA*
And also, Mio Cid's tomb. *Con Dios aquesta lid, yo la
he de arrancar*, he had said: with God's help I shall win.
John Adams had said such many times, too.

Ruy Díaz
EL CID CAMPEADOR, 1040—1090
He of the long beard riding his horse Babieca, with his great sword Colada.

The statue near the *Puente de San Pablo,* Burgos, was made in 1954. El Cid was from Vivar near Burgos. The poetry-loving Adamses were followers of *Don Quixote* and would have heard much in this town of *his* hero, the Cid. Perhaps the Adamses were introduced to *El Poema del Mio Cid* in the three bookstores they visited in Burgos. The poem begins with a young girl of nine years welcoming him:

¡En el nombre del Criador
e del apóstol Sancti Yagile
feridlos, cavalleros...!

Mio Cid Ruy Díaz,
el que en buen ora
cinxó espada

MONASTERIO
de Rodilla, Ermita de
San Marcos del Valle
Jan. 12, 1780
...which is four leagues from Burgos
thence to Briviesca, which is four more.

Santiago, Burgos Cathedral

In the Cathedral in Burgos: Don Quixote uncovered the image of the patron saint of the Spains seated on horeseback...called Don Saint James (Santiago), one of the bravest saints and knights the world ever had or heaven has now.

Don Quixote...descubrió la imagen del patrón de las Españas a caballo...Éste se llama don San Diego, uno de los más valientes santos y caballeros que tuvo el mundo y tiene ahora el cielo. DQ II, 58

TUTOR THAXTER MEETS PEERLESS DULCINEA
that never-enough-celebrated Paragon of Beauty and Gentility
Thaxter to *AA*, May 17, 1780

Her name is Dulcinea, her country El Toboso, a village in La Mancha, her rank must be at least that of a princess...her hair is gold, her eyebrows rainbows, her eyes suns, her cheeks roses, her teeth pearls...

Su nombre es Dulcinea; su patria, El Toboso, un lugar de La Mancha; su calidad, por lo menos, ha de ser de princesa...sus cabellos son oro...sus cejas arcos de cielo, sus ojos soles, sus mejillas rosas, sus labios corales, perlas sus dientes...DQ I,13

So sweet a name.

We struggled patiently and perseveringly, like resolute Pilgrims...*Thaxter* to *AA,* May 17 and June 18, 1780

**SANTA MARÍA
de BRIVIESCA,** Jan. 12, 1780
We passed through several villages
this day and rode along a river and
arrived at Brivisesca. The country
a little more hilly than for
some time past. The
tavern we are in is
a large house and
they gave us
clean sheets.

PANCORBO, Jan 13, 1780

I never saw so beautiful a sight in all my life. JQA

Rode from Briviesca to Pancorbo where we dined. Pancorbo is at the beginning of the rocks. There is the appearance of an ancient carriage way, up the steepest part of the rocks. We passed between two rows of mountains consisting wholly of rocks, the most lofty and craggy precipices that I ever saw. These rocky mountains made the boundary between the ancient Castile and Biscay. Pancorbo is the last village in Old Castile. Here the road parts, to Vitoria and to Bilbao. *JA* We determined to go to Bilbao. *JQA*

Both Mountains, Woods, and Hills, and Rocks,
And Gaming Goats, and fleecy Flocks,
And lowing Herds, and piping Swains,
Come dancing to me o'er the Plains.
Dr. Swift

A KNIGHT-ERRANT

A knight shows to advantage arrayed in glittering armor, pacing the lists before the ladies in some joyous tournament, and all those knights show to advantage that entertain, divert, and, if we may say so, honor the courts of their princes by warlike exercises, or what resemble them. But to greater advantage than all these does a knight-errant show when he traverses deserts, solitudes, crossroads, forests, and mountains in quest of perilous adventures, bent on bringing them to a happy and successful issue... *DQ II, 17*

Bien parece un caballero, armado de resplandecientes armas, pasar la tela en alegres justas delante de las damas, y bien parecen todos aquellos caballeros que en ejercicios militares, o que lo parezcan, entretienen y alegran, y, si se puede decir, honran las cortes de sus príncipes. Pero sobre todos éstos parece mejor un caballero andante, que por los desiertos, por las soledades, por las encrucijadas, por las selvas y por los montes anda buscando peligrosas aventuras, con intención de darles dichosa y bien afortunada cima...
    DQ II,17

San Millán near
ESPEJO in ÁLAVA
Jan. 13, 1780
We passed four leagues from Pancorbo to Espejo where we lodged in the best inn we met with in Spain. Jan. 14 We set out from Espejo about sunrise and dined at Orduña, a considerable village situated with a few smaller ones on a glade of land lying at the foot of the mountains. *Dana*

To look back and recollect the adventures of myself and my wife and daughter and sons, I see a kind of romance, which...would equal anything in the Days of Chivalry or Knight Errantry. *JA, Feb. 10, 1795*

ROAD FROM ESPEJO TO ORDUÑA, Jan. 14, 1780
Four leagues

The road is made all the way, at a great expense, but the descent of the mountains of Orduña is a great curiosity. These mountains are chiefly rocks, of a vast height: but a road has been blown out of the rocks, from the height of the mountains, quite down into the valley. After winding round and round a great way, and observing the marks of the drills remaining in the rocks, the road at last came to a steep where the only method of making a road for a carriage up and down is by serpentining it thus:

HOW TO FIND GOOD FORTUNE

Be moderate in thy sleep, for he who does not rise early does not get the benefit of the day; and remember, Sancho, diligence is the mother of good fortune, and indolence, its opposite, never yet attained the object of an honest ambition

Sea moderando tu sueño; que el que no madruga con el sol, no goza el día; y advierte, ¡oh Sancho!, que la diligencia es madre de la buena ventura; y la pereza, su contraria, jamás llegó al término que pide un buen deseo. DQ II,43

I'll show you the way... Read six hours a day. *Dr. Swift*

ORDUÑA, THE CAPITAL OF BISCAY, Jan. 14, 1780

This morning we set away at about sun rise. We came two leagues and then went a league up hill and then went another league down hill. This was a road made through a mountain I suppose 300 feet in height and all the way almost perpendicular...We dined at Orduña, a little city with gates. *JQA*

They were now in northeastern Spain; the great painter Goya had lived in Aragon, just a little to the south. Born to a Basque family in Saragossa, for five years he had painted designs in Madrid for the Royal Tapestry Factory. Work there stopped late this year because Spain needed the money instead to support America in the war. Goya then went back to paint in Saragossa. The *aguadoras* here, lady water carriers, are from Goya. Water jars were different in each city. *Ed.*

LUYANDO BRIDGE, Jan. 14, 1780

In the afternoon, we followed the road, which pursues the course of a little river, which origi-nates in the mountains of Orduña and rode down between two rows of mountains to Luyando, where we put up for the night, four leagues from Bilbao. We have met great numbers of mules loaded with merchandise from Bilbao. The mules and their drivers look very well. Their burdens are salted fish, sardines, cod and a sort of fish that we see here very plenty called *besugo*. They also carry horse shoes, ready made in Bilbao, to sell in various parts of the kingdom.

We walked one third of the way. *JA*, Feb. 23, 1780

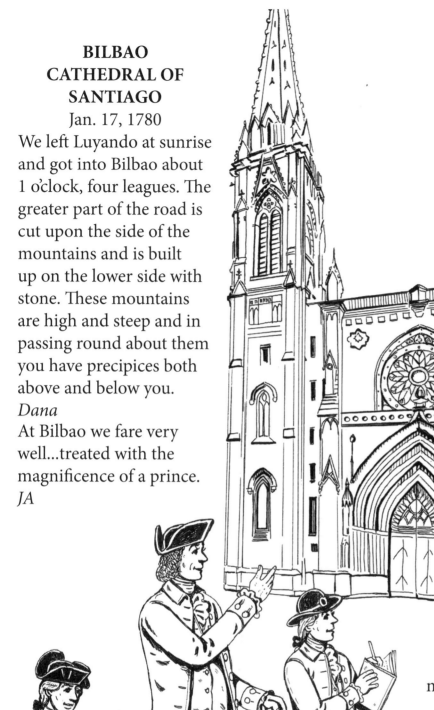

BILBAO CATHEDRAL OF SANTIAGO

Jan. 17, 1780

We left Luyando at sunrise and got into Bilbao about 1 o'clock, four leagues. The greater part of the road is cut upon the side of the mountains and is built up on the lower side with stone. These mountains are high and steep and in passing round about them you have precipices both above and below you.
Dana

At Bilbao we fare very well...treated with the magnificence of a prince.
JA

The town is surrounded with mountains. The tavern where we are is situated between a church and a monastery. We have been entertained with the music of the convent since our arrival. We went to the old parish church of St. Iago, which was certainly standing in the year 1300.

Jan. 18: We spent the day in perambulating the town, through every street. (Had they made this stroll 230 years later, they would have found on the GranVía a wonderful statue of John Adams.)

WE RODE OUR MULES FROM BILBAO, Jan. 20, 1780

We left Bilbao on the afternoon of the 20th of January; there we dismissed our carriages and for great expedition rode our mules through the mountains. We passed the river which divides the two kingdoms and entered that of France at 10 o'clock of the 23rd of January. *Dana*

I wish for a painter to draw me and my Company mounted on muleback...*JA*, Feb. 23, 1780

The habits of a vigorous mind are formed in contending with difficulties. All history will convince you of this. Great necessities call out great virtues. You owe your existence among a people who have made a glorious defense of their invaded Liberties, and who, aided by a generous and powerful ally (France), with the blessing of heaven will transmit this inheritance to ages unborn.

And to
My Dear Charles,
A young adventurer indeed, papa wrote that you made as good a sailor as your brother. At school you must be very attentive to your books, and to every branch of knowledge and improvement. Let your ambition lead you to make yourself master of what you undertake, do not be content to lag behind others, but strive to excel. Your ever affectionate mother.
Abigail Adams

Santa María del Coro
SAN SEBASTIÁN
Capital of Guipuzcoa,
where low taxes =
prosperity.
Jan. 20, 1780

I have traced
and followed
you upon the
maps through
all your pere-
grinations.
It has been a
pilgrimage
indeed. *AA*
April 15, 1780

FUENTERRABÍA, Jan. 20, 1780

In our course we saw a few villages & particularly Fuenterrabía at a distance. We reached St. Jean de Luz, the first village in France, and there we dined.

Biscay, Guipúzcoa, and Álava, three free provinces whose laws the kings of Spain have been sworn to observe, have attracted almost the whole of the American trade because the king has no custom house nor officers here, and there are no duties to be paid. The high and independent spirit of the people has induced the Spanish nation and their kings to respect the ancient liberties of these people.